Library of Congress Cataloging-in-Publication Data:

Bruna, Dick.
    Dick Bruna's picture word book.

    SUMMARY: Alphabetically organized pictures, labeled with one word, present concepts such as counting, opposites, and basic shapes.
    1. Picture dictionaries, English—Juvenile literature. 2. Vocabulary—Juvenile literature. [1. Picture dictionaries] I. Title. II. Title: Picture word
book. PE1629.B78 1989 423'.1 88-18371 ISBN: 0-394-82436-9

Printed in Singapore 1 2 3 4 5 6 7 8 9 0

Dick Bruna's
Picture Word Book

Random House
New York

Aa

apples

airplane

acrobat

armchair

angels

B b

bees

basket

brush

boat

bathtub

blocks

building

beads

broom

bookcase

bread

Bb

butterflies

bunny

banana

bench

balloon

boots

bird

bucket

bugle

ball

bicycle

bear

Cc

car

candy

crayon

castle

cup

clock

clown

circus

Cc

coat

cowboy

cows

chair

couch

camel

carrots

crib

candles

Dd

dancing

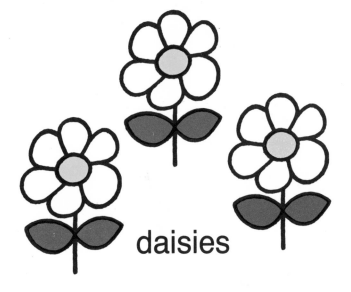

daisies

duck

digging

driving

dustpan

drums

dog

doll

dress

dinner

E e

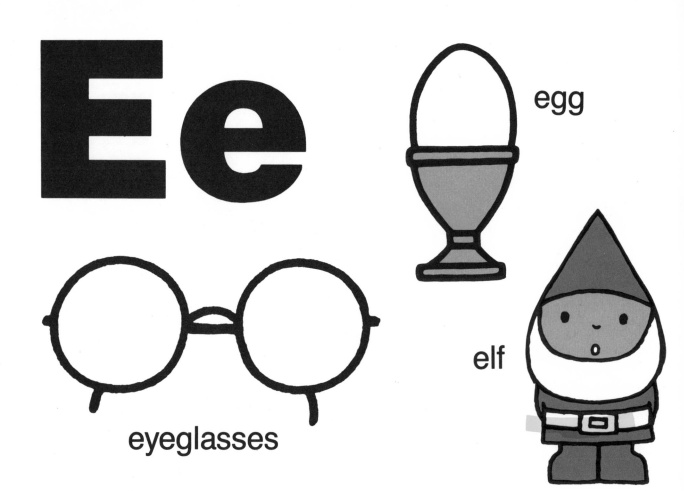

egg

eyeglasses

elf

eskimos

eating

elephants

Ff

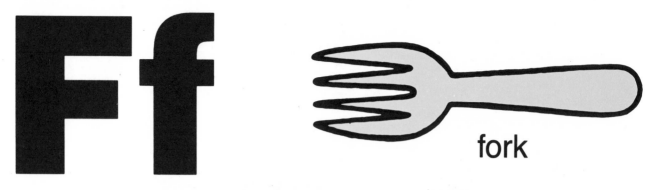

fork

family

feathers

fence

frogs

fish

flute

forest

Ff

farm

Gg

grapes

giraffes

glass

guitar

garden

Hh

hammer

hive

harp

house

hen

hanger

hats

hippo

horse

hoe

Ii

ivy

ice cream

insect

ice

ice skating

Jj

jacket

jam jar

juggling

jump rope

jumping

Kk

kites

knight

kitten

key

knife

king

kangaroos

Ll

lemon

lambs

laundry

lamp

lion

leaves

lighthouse

Mm

moon

mice

mushrooms

measure

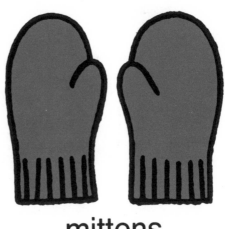

mittens

monkeys

maze

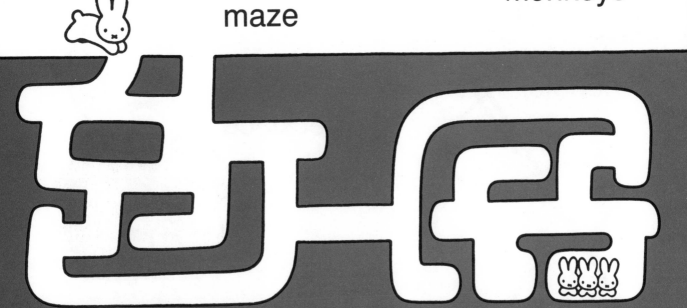

Nn

nest

net

needle

necklace

Oo

owls

oranges

octopus

Oo

orchestra

Pp

pears

pliers

peas

pelican

puppets

policeman

parrots

pencils

puzzle

penguins

pointing

parade

Qq

queen

Rr

raking

rhinoceros

rowing

raining

riding

rabbits

rolling pin

radishes

Ss

scarecrow

seal

shorts

snake

scissors

sailor

sliding

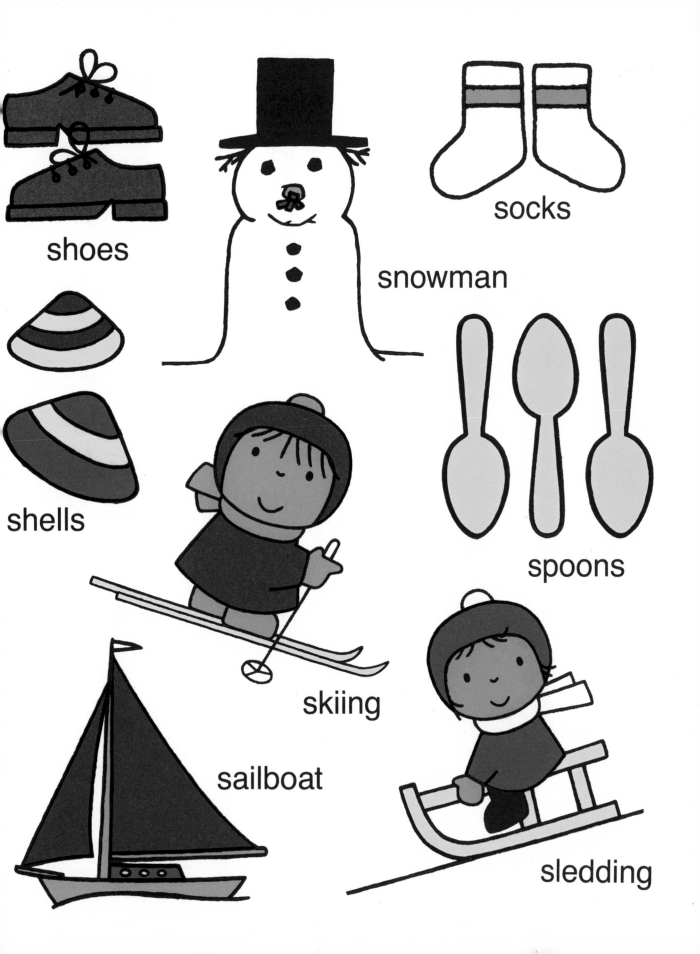

shoes

snowman

socks

shells

skiing

spoons

sailboat

sledding

Ss

sweater

swinging

strawberry

swan

shower

swimming

Tt

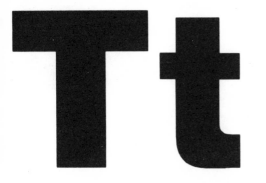

tent

 tightrope

tigers

T t

turtles

towel

teapot

top

tennis

telephone

table

truck

Uu

uniform

underwear

umbrella

Vv

violin

W w

walrus

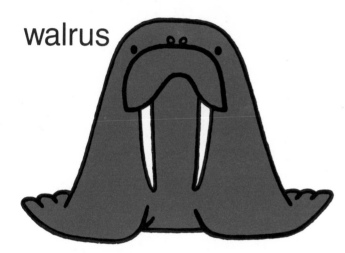

watering

whistle

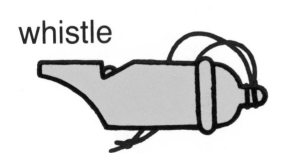

wheelbarrow

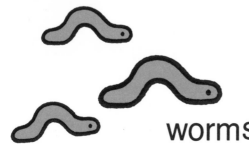

worms

Ww

watering
can

wheelchair

whale

washing

Xx

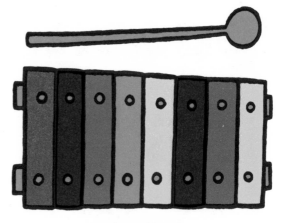

xylophone

yacht

Yy

Zz

zebra

Opposites

asleep   awake

big   little

front   back

happy

sad

up

down

grown ups

baby

Opposites

in

out

pushing

pulling

open

closed

Shapes

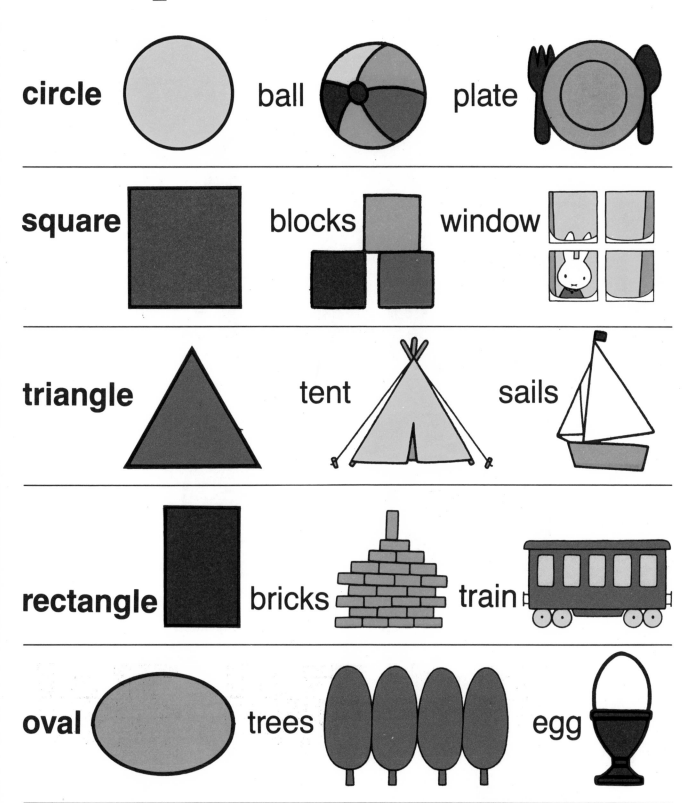

circle   ball   plate

square   blocks   window

triangle   tent   sails

rectangle   bricks   train

oval   trees   egg

Counting

1
one

2
two

3
three

4 four

5 five

6 six

7 seven

8 eight

9 nine

10 ten